Quilt Pieces

To Kathy,
Peace & Blessings!

Quilt Pieces

POEMS

by

MARY WILLETTE HUGHES

Mary Willette Hughes

NORTH STAR PRESS OF ST. CLOUD, INC.

ISBN: 0-87839-174-6

First Edition

Cover photo:
Life in the Margins #2: After Autumn
Wall Quilt by Caryl Bryer Fallert, Oswego, Illinois

Printed in the United States of America by
Versa Press, Inc.
East Peoria, Illinois 61611

Published by
North Star Press of St. Cloud, Inc.
P.O. Box 451
St. Cloud, Minnesota 56302-0451

ACKNOWLEDGEMENTS

The poems in *Quilt Pieces* were improved by many poet-teachers, readers, and friends during the last ten years, but especially deep gratitude is given to Dr. Eva Hooker, C.S.C., and to Dr. Nancy Hynes, O.S.B., English faculty at the College of St. Benedict and St. John's University, for their teaching expertise, generous encouragement, and vital friendship. I also thank my husband, Mark, thoughtful first reader, and the editors who have published my work.

LIFE IN THE MARGINS #2: AFTER AUTUMN
QUILT DESIGN: CONCEPT AND PROCESS
BY CARYL BRYER FALLERT

"At least once each year, I make a scrap quilt from strips of fabric left over from other quilt projects. The leftover strips from these quilts are sewn together in groups of related colors. The black overlaid design is based on one of my notebook-margin "doodle" designs (thus the title), which was enlarged and appliquéd to the pieced background. All the machine quilting was done free-hand, with no marking, and it echoes the doodle design of the black appliqué. This quilt was begun in December of 1988 and completed in February of 1989."

This book is dedicated to:

my mother, Florence, poet and watercolor artist
my father, Don, a wise man who loved and worked the land

CREDITS

The following poems in *Quilt Pieces* were originally published in the listed journals:

"Visitation," *Lower Stumpf Lake Review*, Vol. XXIX, May 1994; the *National Catholic Reporter*, September 29, 2000.

"Nursing Home Bath," *Voices*, 1996.

"In My Mother's House," *Voices*, 1996.

"Storm," Originally titled as "What Linneaus Said in the Philosophia Botanica," *Lower Stumpf Lake Review*, Vol. XXXI, May 1996.

"Farmhouse for Rent," *North Coast Review*, Spring 1997.

"Faint Green Fragrance," Originally titled "In Their Fortieth Year of Marriage," *Loonfeather*, Vol. 17, No. 2, 1997.

"Beyond the Stillness," *Studio One*, May 1997.

"Any Monday," *Lower Stumpf Lake Review*, Vol. XXXIII, May 1998.

"The Day My Father Died," *Lower Stumpf Lake Review*, Vol. XXXIII, May 1998.

"October at Bluefin Bay," *1997 Minnesota Poetry Calendar*, Black Hat Press.

"Mother, Your Picture Dated 1973," *1998 Minnesota Poetry Calendar*, Black Hat Press.

"Grandfather's Visit," *Studio One,* Spring 1999.

"The Shadow Loom," *North Coast Review*, Winter 1999.

"The Poet," *The Moccasin*, League of Minnesota Poets Publication, 1999.

"Will Death Be This," *Studio One*, Spring 2001.

"Lines for a Husband," Florence Hynes Willette, *Shadows and Light*, North Star Press, 1969.

GRANT

—$2000 Individual Artist in Poetry grant from the Central Minnesota Arts Board in 1998.

ADDITIONAL PUBLICATIONS

—Poems have also appeared in the following literary magazines and anthologies: *Nostalgia, Anthology of Space and Sky, Diotima, Native West Press, Sisters Today, The Moccasin,* and *Divine Favor: The Art of Joseph O'Connell, Liturgical Press.*

Table of Contents

A Story Quilt xv

I. The Shadow Loom

II. The Turning of Days

III. Going Home

A STORY QUILT

The thread of life
unspools

        from the mind of God, joining you
        to me and we to all, like thread in my
        mother's hands stitching bits of beauty

into unity
Day by day

        she follows lightly penciled marks on
        on calico cloth, creating a quilt design
        patterned in prism colors of sun-yellow
        joy and shadow-blue sorrow, revealing

a life
twice told

        Her quilt grows fragile, is cherished
        as heirloom in my cedar chest, yet, when
        I remove it, hold it, unfold it, her story

lives again
transcends

The Shadow Loom

FARMHOUSE FOR RENT

February 1923

I

I imagine my father striding through the porch
and turning right to enter the vacant farm house.

On the table, thick with dust, last fall's flowers
have shriveled brown in a green fruit jar.

A wood cook stove and sink
with iron-handled pump on the north wall,

a set of French windows to the west,
   she will like them

and straight ahead, empty pantry shelves.

   Yes, after the wedding,
   hard work.
   This will do.

II

I imagine my mother pausing to study the fieldstone porch.
someday I will write a poem about shaped endurance

She sees the kitchen table where they will come for meals.
a vase of flowers here, phlox and sweet peas, perhaps

Opening the wood stove's large gray oven door she thinks.
this spill-charred oven needs to be deep cleaned

Beyond smudged French windows, a gnarled boxelder tree.
someday, at dusk, I will paint a watercolor of this tree

Empty pantry shelves wait like blank canvas.
shelves will fill with canned tomatoes, corn, beans

Yes, after the wedding,
hard work.
This will do.

EARTH, AIR, FIRE, AND WATER
June 1932

I watch myself, a baby, sleeping in a wicker
laundry basket near the warm kitchen stove.

I do not see the table bright with daisies
and nasturtiums picked by my mother,

nor the opened cook stove oven, crusty
with a bubbled patch of peach pie spill,

nor a gray enamel sink with curved-handled
pump that raises water to our drinking pail,

nor French windows above the kitchen sink,
tugged open to smell fresh-cut alfalfa,

nor pantry shelves, lined with rows
of garden colors, shiny in clear glass jars.

I do not know I am in a kitchen where
work, riddled with love, is as sure as:

cinnamon caramel rolls after Sunday Mass,
Pine-Sol scented air during spring cleaning,

cook stove fires stoked with dried corncobs,
well water carried to the new strawberry bed.

I do not know my work. I will learn.

ONLY THE DARK

Sitting in the high chair
at noon meal near the threshing crew, I am playing
with my Cracker Jack prize . . . a capped whistle.

I blow softly,
like the sound of a mourning dove, smell fried chicken
and raspberry pie, hear sounds of men joking, talking bushels
per acre and the clink of silverware against Blue Willow.

I inhale deeply;
the whistle cap lodges, far down my throat, stuck;
I cannot breathe in or out.

It grows dark,
like the sun gone down behind the barn,
like Mama closing the door after we pray,
    . . . *if I should die before I wake* . . .

They say I turned bluish-purple, arms flailing; they say
my father tipped his chair backwards; they say his eyes
blazed like lightning bolts; they say he grabbed my arms,
lifted, turned me up-side-down like a rag doll; they say
he beat on my back with the thick fist of his hand.

I only remember the dark.

GRANDFATHER'S VISIT
1936

I am four and stand near
the hot kitchen wood stove.

Air from the opened oven
warms my naked body.

I sway gracefully as corn
leaves in a July breeze

and wait for my bath
in the aluminum washtub.

A knock on the door.
Grandfather sees, shouts,

You get your clothes on!
I run like Eve

from his loud, stern
voice. Crouched

in the dark, I learn
how cold shame is.

LET GO, SHE SAID
1936

My thin, pregnant mother stands
warming herself above the hot air
register in the white-breath dawn
of our farm home.

A printed, blue-flowered dress billows,
bell-shaped, like a floating kite riding air
above the coal-stoked furnace below.

I catch and hug her dress tight
around her knees; legs, covered
with cotton stockings colored like
brown sugar, are nubby-rough and hot.

I look up but cannot see her face.
I feel the round, blue mound
of new baby blocking my sight.

Let go, she says,
and draws away.

I am alone.
Running back, I climb into my still
warm bed, spread with Mama's
handmade, Sun Bonnet Sue, quilt.

I find my teddy
and hold him close.

THE SHADOW LOOM

She sits in the small glow
of a kerosene lamp,
a Rembrandt painting.

While children sleep
and husband is away,
writing fills her

silence. I wake,
a child listening
from shadows

to the sound of my mother
telling her poems
to the dark;

· the rise and fall of her voice
weaving
in and out of me.

A TASTE FOR READING
1938

It is the first day of first grade in the one-room
country school. Miss Agnes holds a shiny white
card with a picture of clustered, ripe grapes.

I think about the smell of sun-warmed grapes,
biting through tough skin, sweet juice
flooding my mouth, and the crunch
of slippery, small seeds.

Teacher's eyes look straight at me.
She asks, *What color are the grapes?*

Purple, I say.

She points to the letters on the bottom
of the card.
You said this word, Mary.

I whisper the word with my lips,
taste "purple" on my tongue
and begin to own the world
of words with my eyes.

FARM FIRE
Friday, October 12, 1939, 8:30 p.m.

Downstairs, in my parents' bed
under layers of thick quilts,
I shiver, stare out the window

Mama's face frightened;
she covers my eyes, but I see
fire arc toward our house

Red yellow orange flames
cut the night jagged, spill
over the machine shed roof

Showers of sparks burst
the dark into a million eyes
coming straight at me

Silhouette men form a line,
move in rhythm, pass buckets
of water from the windmill

Smoke snakes the open
window, hovers the bed,
crawls under my covers

I know the feel of fear
sliding up my body,
coiling round my throat

AFTER A DOWNPOUR

drenches the farm, sun baptizes
the world in topaz-yellow light. My young soul rises
to the rainbow curving a slate-blue sky.

Bare feet sink in the rain-rutted lane. I watch
a Holstein herd across the barbed wire fence; placid
eyes stare back at me, dark as mystery. They stand
alone . . . together,
do not rest their heads on one another's necks
like horses, do not stand swishing tails to keep
flies from another's eyes. They simply stand
alone . . . together.
Time stops,   carves my memory deep
as gravestone words.

Whenever a rainbow paints after-days, I return
here, where my soul first rose to the rainbow
and feet marked the mud of earth.

THE HONORED GUEST

On every upholstered chair in the old house, Gramma
pinned layers of washable, store-bought antimacassars,
a protection against skin oil and everyday farm soil.

I loved to lean way, way back in Grampa's overstuffed
chair, smooth the rumpled antimacassars, and imagine
myself grown and great and grand as Grampa.

My fingers liked to poke, wiggling through ecru lace
to lift, to look below, to stroke the chair's plush velvet
fabric: unsoiled, unworn and still brand-new beautiful.

Knowing the priest was coming, Gramma removed all
antimacassars, except the last. There she displayed her
own creation, a meticulous star design, flawlessly made.

AUGUST LITURGY, 1942

liturgy: people's work

Threshing day begins for Mama at first light.
She lifts a cornflower-blue, bib apron over dark
braided hair and mixes yeast bread for baking.

Men in hayracks, pulled by teams of draft horses,
gather shocks of ripened oats from the north field
and pitchfork them into the mouth of the roaring,

mysterious, threshing machine. It swallows and
separates grain from golden stems, blowing
a straw stack, high and wide by day's end.

Mama said I am to pick and shuck garden peas
for the noon meal. In the hammock, under shade
of weeping willow, my thumb cracks the pods,

pushes peas to ping the saucepan. I crunch
empty pods, suck the sweet, stringy, green juice.
Mama said the pan must be filled to the brim.

It is noon. I smell crusty loaves of baked honey-
wheat and hear chicken sizzle in cast iron. Men
wash up outside, rinse sweat and straw chaff

from face, hands and arms. They gather at table.
My peas steam in a white bowl.   A silent prayer.
One by one, the men take and eat Mama's bread.

PEACH PIES

My mother, Dutch, voted best pie baker in Prescott Township
by threshing crews, stands at our 8:00 a.m. kitchen counter.
She calls me from playing with my kitten as she lifts an apron
over her head like a vestment and says, "It's pie time."

The pies began yesterday at Lubitz Grocery in Delavan.
She taught me how to press my thumb against the fruit flesh
that must always "give a little" and be that one particular shade
of color, that one particular scent of ripe.

I watch her roll out six pie crusts, peel and divide each peach
in half, remove the pit, put it in her mouth, suck bits of pulp
and juice, sweeter than wine. She gives me every other pit.
Peaches mix with sugar, flour, spices, and a splash of almond.

Pies are in the Monarch oven, cooked by burning dried corn
cobs from the wood box. An aroma, like morning incense,
breathes through every room of the farmhouse. Baked golden
brown, thick juice oozes from steam vents in the top crust.

Cooling on wire racks, pies wait for the gathering of threshers.
I help serve Mama's fried chicken and mashed potato dinner.
And now . . . dessert. We watch each man lift and eat forkfuls
of our warm, flaky-crust peach pie.   The liturgy is complete.

THE INVITATION

I never got to do fun things like my five brothers 'cause "I was a girl,"
'cause I had to do "girl work," had to help Mama in the house.

> I never got to rope-swing
> in the haymow and free-fall fifty feet
> like a dropped rock, plummeting to the haylake below;
>
> never got to stay up late
> catching leghorn pullets under October's moon
> hanging in the sky, crisp as frost and white as a street light;
>
> never got to drive the mares,
> Lil and Doll, pulling the full manure spreader
> through a corn-stubble field, spinning joy-juice over the earth;
>
> never got to watch
> when Grampa Oliver brought the dapple-gray stallion,
> Prince, to the north grove to "service" my filly, Morning Star.
>
> My dad caught me peeking from behind the granary and shouted,
> YOU GIT TO THE HOUSE !
> What was that all about?

But one boring, August day, the brothers did invite me to join them. We
thwacked rotten eggs against a grunting, wallowing sow's bristly back!

THE KISS
September, 1943

Late afternoon. We two sixth grade girls walk a gravel road
    on the way home from District 32 Country School.

Genevieve Eisenschenk, tall, gangly, world wise, turns
    and asks, Do you know what a French kiss is? I don't,

but, since I'm half French and half Irish, I think I ought to know.
    We stop in the middle of the road, drop our books.

Hands grip my shoulders and open mouthed, she kisses
    my mouth; her tongue invades, tastes of garlic sausage,

tunnels past my lips, my teeth, straight to my tongue!
    I shudder, push her away, spit my mouth dry twice,

rush home to the bathroom, wash my tongue with Lava
    soap, brush my teeth with Mama's mix of soda/salt and . . .

chew two sticks of Black Jack licorice gum.
                               I think I will only be Irish!

STORM

late Friday afternoon - morning wash damp
on the clothesline - sultry air licks
our skin - Mother glances north
toward Mankato cliffs - dark
sky roiling hungry - three
blackberry clouds ex-
tend funnel ends
vortex roars
rotates
stings
and
su
c
k
s

SHE IS ALONE

A knock. She is alone in the farmhouse
the summer of her twelfth birthday.

The hired man's brother and his friend
say they've come to visit. She is flattered.

On the couch, they sit close beside her,
press her arms tight against her body.

Man hands move on each breast, touch
her nipples;   her face flushes;

an unknown body pulse wakens, throbs.
They do not speak, they do not look at her.

A long time and they leave. A long time
she stays there.   They must love her.

Later, she rides her bike to them,
filled with this sweet secret,   this joy

in their love.   They do not speak,
they do not look at her.   They turn away.

Silence storms her, echoes like thunder
in her soul; tears sting like sleet.

AFTER THE ANNIVERSARY PARTY
1944

I am thirteen and shocked.

Counting months and years
I discover my first cousin
born before his parents
were married nine months.

You mean?

Mama said . . . *It happens
to the best of us.*

MY MOTHER AND *A FEW FIGS FROM THISTLE*

I

Husband and hired men are back at winter farm work,
her kitchen chores are finished and now,
she owns this quiet.

She holds Edna St.Vincent's Millay's book:
thin, well-worn, corners carefully
turned back, like time.

Fireplace logs flame and crackle. Cypress paneled
walls, deeply grooved, listen again
for the sound of her voice

as she reads aloud. Her fingertips touch music
in the line, ear delights in rhyme,
mind in the sonnet turn.

Beneath the book in her lap, she lifts a scribbled
writing pad and sharpened pencil.
She begins again . . .

continued

II

LINES FOR A HUSBAND

Florence Hynes Willette

I look at you with deeper, clearer eyes
Than once I looked. The pattern of your ways
Is known to me. From out the flexuous maze
Of our shared years, I know why you are wise.
I know why sometimes after family prayer
When dreams have hushed the children's revelry,
You come to lean your head against my knee
And wordless, call my fingers to your hair.

Your faults are my dear secret; soberly
I lock them in the cupboard of my life,
Aware of kinship old as Adam's wife
In those fair bonds that hold you one with me.
A girl's beloved moves godlike in her sight . . .
A woman knows his shadows and his light.

THE POET

moves
down the hall

of night, driven
by need

like a bird of prey
gliding, sightless

in flight,
listening

for rustling
in the underbrush

THE WINDMILL

for my father

The old windmill stands straight
and strong, a sentinel on a hill
near the weathered farmhouse.

Spinning in wind, the working
fins hum a steady, low-pitched
psalming as the windmill pole

thrusts down, then up
with start-and-stop breath,
drawing clear, pure water

from hallowed ground
like organ pipes
that flow with music.

BENEATH THE PEAR TREE

Late September sun lazes the afternoon air, yet
beneath the pear tree, our front lawn buzzes alive.

Overripe pears scatter across the still-green grass
like small graves. They have fallen and fallen
though we pick them daily with a long-handled
wire basket, careful not to bruise pale yellow flesh.

Honey bees, carpenter bees, wasps, bumble bees
burrow pear pulp and consume fermented juice.
A sticky glaze gleams on groggy, heavy-laden
bodies, climbing and falling from grass stems,
teeter-tottering on twigs. Leaning down I hear
them droning and think, ah . . . they hum
little drinking songs of harvest.

A soft thud. I pick up the newly fallen pear, bite
freckled tough skin, suck its pulp. Juice trickles
down my chin and wrist. I lick nectar-sweet skin.
Trailing my hand through thick sun-warmed grass,

a honey bee crawls languorously up my finger . . .
perhaps . . . for petting.   Sudden fire stings.

MINNESOTA CASH CROP

Faribault County fields roll thick, green-gold

carpets of soybeans over rich, flat-back land.

September's scudding clouds throw shadow-

frost across long, straight rows. Early beans

already wither, desert-dry. Their stalks stand

knee-high, look naked without leaves. Crisp

short hair covers brittle pods that crack open

under thumb and finger. They house one-eyed,

ecru beans that wait for birth by combine. If

hail, grasshoppers, purple seed stain, root-rot,

flood, blight, cocklebur, mosaic leaf, early

frost, white mold and nematode are fenced out

and last fall's contracts for the soybean futures

were fenced in,   perhaps,   a harvest of green.

A PLACE OF GRACE

The first and only time I hear my mother say,
you possess the best qualities of your father and me,

I am stunned.　　　　Daily my full-length mirror
speaks its harsh adolescence truth, yet . . .

something within me dives headlong
into my mother's clearest, deepest, bluest vision . . .

a secret, sacred place
I will return to all my days.

There, closed eyes open
to an amazing azure air embracing me.

There, I breathe within the gaze
of my mother's blue eyes.

WHITE GARDENIAS

I have grown learned in sorrow.
                     Li Ch'ing-chao

I

Wednesday night
you drive me home,
my arm under your shirt,
skin smooth, fragrant
as white gardenias

Your ring on my finger,
a promise of new joy
We breathe good night

II

Friday morning
a phone call
My parents stand
in my room,
something nameless
between them shatters
their faces, broken
glass whispers

Chuck drowned last night
combined oats all day
drove to the pond
dove off the dock
came up underneath
hit his head
friends said
no one noticed
he did not surface

III

Beyond my window
sunlight floods
black
against green ash leaves

Eighteen
and like an ocean shell
cast ashore
I am hollow
with this wound

IV

In after days,
the presence of his absence
resounds empty rooms,
asleep, awake

I trace the contours of pain
in a kinship
that proves I still live

Fragrant white gardenias,
withered brown . . .
my life

I touch that day
after betrothal,
when my other self drowned
and do not believe
love will come green again
and flower

The Turning of Days

BLIND DATE
Valentine Dance

He is tall, dark-haired and Irish
with a scholarly, shy reserve.

It is "like-at-first-look" for me.
A snail-paced year of waiting . . .

he calls for a second date . . .
then another . . . and another.

I see, *as through a glass darkly*.

The mourning veil lifts and a light
path beckons. He designs my ring

carved with Alpha and Omega;
we exchange plain gold bands.

A blind date opened my eyes
to new vision.

BEYOND THE STILLNESS

Thick fog and lake water meld
to an absolute gray and wait
like closed eyes for morning

sun to rise and simmer the air,
opening a palette of summer
colors: the full, rich greens

of canopied leaves, ripe gold
of wheat edging the lake, hot
blue of cloudless July sky.

Two snowy egrets glide low
over the water in soundless
sync, wing tip to wing tip.

A fish leaps, breaks the surface
glass, and for a moment, time
is reflected in concentric circles.

OCTOBER AT BLUEFIN BAY

From our hillside room we could not view
        white-caps chase to catch the shore,
            nor hear the pounded boulders

sound, nor see a gray-green
        wind sway golden birch trees.
            But from our morning-lit bed

we watched beyond arched windows,
        two slender maples embrace,
            flaring leaves of crimson.

WHAT MAMA WROTE

I never saw my father cry when fire
burned farm buildings to the ground

nor when clouds of hail razored
ripening corn, oat and soybean fields

nor when he was fired in St. Paul
from a government-appointed job

nor when my brother was injured and
cast-bound, waist-to-ankle, for months

nor when he waited for his prodigal son
to drive home, drunk again at two a.m.

nor when he buried his mother, Annie,
and then, his father, Oliver

but when I miscarried, alone, in a far city,
Mama wrote, *your dad cried*

FEBRUARY GIFT

Beyond the hospital window, a muffled, white
    womb world.   All night blizzard snow
swirled into deep drifted curves that glisten now
    in blue-morning sun like sparkled tissue
paper on a birthday gift. After labor's long night,
    you came forth from my womb's liquid
darkness, transforming the season of cold and ice
    and tears, spring below the winter snow.

THE TURNING OF DAYS

there is a convergence of the material and the spiritual
into the Omega Point   Teilhard de Chardin

Seven children are loved into being.

The turning of days forges our spines straight,
strong and supple to bend in the coming winds
of time. Grace blesses us with a mantle of
faith; a seamless, circular garment, woven
daily in the loom of our lives.

We believe we are destined
toward a distant
center.

CHILDREN IN PARADISE

Our seven children, bundled
in crayon bright colors

race out the kitchen door
to be one with first snow.

Young, set free, they shout,
dive deep in ice cream drifts,

rise and fall like ponies
circling on a merry-go round.

They play *Follow-the-Leader*,
from tallest down to small

and tramp a lopsided circle
for a fast *Fox and Goose* chase.

Breathless, they fall back-
wards in unruffled snow;

arms arc and print half circles;
laughter rises on white wings.

TAKING OVER

Look at them! you shout. *You can almost touch them!*
The sky darkens. We hear wings and the resounding

whonk, whonk of Hudson Bay Canada geese. We too
take wing and forget all our day's work and cares.

Over roof tops, tree tops, clouds of geese come and
come, black V's printing a language on the sky.

In high flight, whirring wings never cease moving.
As the point goose of a wedge tires, another senses

its limits, breaks rank, flies forward and takes over.
I think of marriage, of family, of you coming home

after your day, putting on blue plaid shirt and jeans
to take over the care of our seven young children.

ANY MONDAY

I lift wet sheets from automatic washer
to gas dryer and think about Mama's washday . . .

old 1938 Maytag washing machine putt-putts
on the fieldstone porch. Mama's first load,
always whites, churns in Fels-Naphtha suds.

Her chapped red hand pushes a lever that feeds
steaming wash though the wringer's rolling
lips. Flattened laundry slides to a tub of blue

rinse water, swished, then wringer-wrung
again. Whites cascade to a wicker basket
that Mama lugs outside to the clothes line.

Sheets are pinned to taut metal wire; south
wind lifts them high as sails against gray sky
to snap, billow and flap, overlapping lines.

My cousin Nancy and I leave kitchen dishes
undone, sneak outside to play hide-and-seek
between, around, beneath clingy damp sheets.

This Monday night, laundered white linens
dress our marriage bed scented with store-
bought, fabric-sheet fragrance, not fresh air.

Still, after young children sleep into dreams
husband, we will play under tangled sheets.

SON AT THE PIANO

October moon floods the bay window
　　filling the room in a symphony of light,
　　　　Clair de Lune flows like the *Moldau*.

The old piano welcomes his man hands
　　and phrases linger the air like fragrance.
　　　　Always, as he plays, she pauses to listen.

Unwritten melodies channel through
　　slender fingers from a far, magical place,
　　　　distant as crystal stars and as beautiful.

Tonight, he wings his way to Beijing
　　where he will perform the Masters . . . music
　　　　of the centuries, living in his still hands.

ADVICE FOR A DAUGHTER

What your mother tells you now,
in time you will come to know.

Mitsuye Yamade

I saw a shooting star tonight
blaze the corner of my eye,
its luminous trail a dazzling white
like diamond dust across the sky.

Beware of this, my woman-child,
kisses velvet in passion's dark;
Lothario's love flames brilliant, wild
but burns cold, possessing his mark.

COMMON GROUND
ninth grade

He storms, slams out the kitchen door, pot
    and papers shoved in blue plaid pocket.
He seeks a solitude: a place far from us,
    from rooms too small, demands too large.

A night fist fight in the park and he breaks
    a classmate's rib; he comes to table sullen,
skips school again, again the phone rings.
    Money is missing.   He asks for a kitten.

At the Humane Society, I wait in the car
    and notice brown winter grass beginning
to tinge a faint green. He returns carrying
    an all black kitten and names him Mutzi.

Wrapped in the patchwork quilt I made
    for him, he cradles the purring Mutzi.
I am beside him. We stroke the kitten;
    for a brief moment, our hands touch.

MOTHER TO SON

fear crouches
in my midnight room
and springs

I ride this terror . . .
a panther crashing
through frozen land
lost

while you ride
the white horse
powder in alley
rush

chaos
in our lives
like black ink
spilled on a winter
white blotter

TOWARD FLIGHT

Spring Azure butterfly

Our son, long confined in his prison of addiction
aches to be set free. He, like a chrysalis,
feels walls encasing him . . . walls
formed by his other self, his other life.

You emerge, Spring Azure. Iridescent
wings unfold . . . dry . . . flex against
unknown air, pulse with first breath
in the stunning light of rebirth.

Our son trembles on the edge,
pauses . . . chooses . . . opens. Released
from crumbling walls of darkness,
he breathes the clear light of morning.

Rising above the sunned green of spring,
flight on new wings.

THE GIFT GIVEN

He holds me,
    night air fresh
        with lilac fragrance.

Gentle hands ask
    the thickened planes
        of my autumn body;

awakened by his love
    like Eve from sleep, I turn
        naked to my naked husband

and share the answer
    given as gift, as blessing,
        in first spring.

AGAINST YOUR DARKNESS

Winter sun burns black.

Your eyes, remote
as stars, stare hours
of day; without sleep
depression paces you
in room-to-room orbit.

I wake alone, cold,
your covers thrown.
In the dim living room,
you are a shadow
silhouette in your chair.

Lost in another dark
you shiver at my touch.
Kneeling, I hold you,
lead you down the hall,
close the bedroom door

and wait for morning sun.

THE BEAST IS BACK

Last week, I felt it stalking, sniffing
for your scent beyond
the screen door.

Yesterday, I saw it crouching behind
your porch chair,
waiting to spring.

Last night, I heard it howling my silence,
possessing your soul
as you lay curved

on the floor, in broken moonlight.

THIS TRUTH I KNOW

We must go back and find a trail in the ground.
William Stafford

I.

Our words rasp against each other now, sting like the scratch of a thorn and hidden, bleed to the inside.

We are parched loneliness, each a yellow rose withering in waterless glass at opposite ends of the table.

Our days are strewn with brown petals and dry stems, crushed by frozen wills, weary feet. This truth I know.

II.

At dusk we meet, our old place in the park's blooming rose garden, near the winding path.   Hope, a small bud.

There is no trail leading back to days when love's fragrance was so fresh we could breathe it through our skin, yet

hearts may open again, petal by petal, offering seasoned beauty, rich with new with perfume. This truth I know.

MARIPOSA GROVE

They enter the grove; voices

hush.   Each seeks the other's

hand. They study the massive

sequoia tree that began as two,

now grown into one majestic

tree. For hundreds of years

they reached to touch, to join

acres of shallow roots and red-

brown trunks, sending liquid

life to flow through cambium

cells. Far below the blue-green,

spiny-leafed branches, yellow

butterflies rise, swirl, dance.

TRANSITION

The first time I was called Gramma, a heavy
iron bar clang-clanged

across my startled mind like lowered stop arms
at a railroad crossing.

I paused . . . waiting for the train-brain rumble
to fade, the stop bar to rise.

The child took two fingers of my right hand
tightly in his, looked up,

and owned my mutable heart.

MIGRATION

200 hundred million *mariposas monarcas*,   3,000 miles

O Great Spirit, hover above them, delight in your new creation.
O Great Spirit, you provide milkweed, nectar, shelter, and water.

Two little granddaughters, holding hands and laughing, skip down a dirt path between rows of tall, stately evergreens. As the sisters race back and forth, a billowing cloud of monarchs rises behind them, like the wake of a ship. Wings are mosaic-patterned: orange, black and white; bodies weighing less than a dime leave the pines in a swirl of life, like waves of confetti tossed against a copen sky. I hear wing sounds whirring, whispering, soft as rain; watch them soar like flung jewels, saffron-gold dancing in sunlight. Each time the children rush by, butterflies rise, settle, hang, flutter. Their flights call them yearly across a five-generation cycle, to eighteen acres of Mexico's Sierra Madre Mountains where they remain for five months until the cycle begins again. Millions arrive to inhabit the sacred groves and overwinter near November first, the feast of *Dia de los Muertos*, when religious legend says they are souls of the dead, returning to their loved ones.   Sisters, will you return remembering the day monarchs rose up and bowed down for you?

O Great Spirit, protect them from dark storm and daily danger.
O Great Spirit, guide their passage from one world to the next.

VALENTINE'S DAY

Years ago, husband, you brought me a gift,
ribbon tied . . . daffodil bulbs with paper thin

skins, tall stems and trumpets of yellow
gold. Sitting on today's kitchen table,

a single daffodil you picked two days ago
from the circle-garden you planned

and dug and planted late last September.
Plump, unopened, it drooped head-down

but in cool tap water, rose to full flower.
The fresh, forward face, a marvel of angled

architecture and like a ruffled sun it shines,
proclaiming spring on a slender stem.

Husband, you have tended our family
for years; a ring of perennials, deep-rooted.

THE SEASONS OF MARRIAGE

The dawn of our marriage we planted
two sapling sugar maples, his and mine,
twenty feet apart in our front yard.
Our home, newly built, to be shaded
and graced by these partner trees.

Now tall, they touch each other; trunks
measure a foot across. Today, winter
winds brush their bones etching a black
skeleton against metal-gray sky, that

sends skyward artery branches, twig
veins. Again this spring, thousands
of buds will burst into green flames,
flare leaf hands, innumerable as stars.

Years past, a summer storm severed
a third of his tree. Hot, wild winds
hacked the vulnerable north branch
and downed it, leaving an absence,
visible even when foliage is full.

Autumn days, leaves reflect a startling
butterscotch light. Liquid gold flows
eastern windows, floods childless rooms
with sweet yellow song and for one
crowning week, amazes October eyes.

It is the twilight of our marriage;
the shade trees tower, ample, with deep
roots. Heavenward their leaves and
branches interweave, reaching still.

Going Home

APRIL COMES COLD

on north wind breath, yet finches return early

to flutter our highest maple limbs, unraveling

red-throated song like spooled ribbon flung

across the dawn. Yet, I am as fallow ground,

frozen . . . our son lost in a storm of addiction.

Turning homeward, I journey back, yearning

to see the wet, black fields of winter wheat

coming green.

My mother opens the farmhouse door, singing.

DECADES PASSED

As they drive gravel roads
the ten-minutes to town,
Blue Earth or Winnebago,
rosaries surface: rattling,
untangling from Dad's bib
overall pocket and Mom's
jumbled, carryall purse.

Antiphonal voices slide
along the beads, racing
at 55 miles an hour.

Hmmm, let's see now . . .
that's ten miles
and sixty-five prayers
at fifty-five miles per hour
for ten minutes equals . . .
perhaps . . .
a salvation equation.

REMINDERS AND QUESTIONS

In early marriage
his little reminders and questions:
> *hurry up, let's not be late for church*
> *why did you trump my ace*
> *did you get the part for the tractor*
vexed her to expressions of exasperation
bubbling up like Yellowstone's sulfur pots,
until they burst forth.

In late marriage
his little questions and reminders:
> *is your seat belt buckled*
> *did you get your nap*
> *remember to take your pills*
evoke her daily thanks, rising and resting
on kitchen air like the fragrance of yeast
bread, freshly baked.

I SPEAK TO YOU, MALIGNANCY

Without warning
          your cells spindle wildly,

weaving flesh and bone.
          Silently, stealthily, you

lock pinpoint teeth
          and ravenous, grow . . .

a white bud flowering
          in gray, x-ray shadows.

You crowd and strangle
          life to feed your own.

Spring will not come
          green for her, bearing

fragrant hyacinths;
          snowflakes will swirl

her grave like plum
          blossoms, stormed.

MOTHER, WHERE HAVE YOU GONE

New thought fails and falls in your brain, lost forever like a mountain
climber who loses hold and in slow motion, tumbles to a deep crevasse.

Over and over you say, *I want to go home* . . . but you have lived here,
this house, for forty-four years. We drive you to your birth-home, yet

restless as a caught moth you flutter about the house. Again and again
you pull back lace living room curtains to stare and stare at nowhere.

Last week you ran away, down elm-lined streets, west on the gravel road
past the Baptist Home. We found you, wandering, murmuring, *Mama.*

Will time take me to your place, hovering above this cusp of death?
Fears rise; hollow bones clatter down my midnight in a chilling dance.

You are prisoner of complicated locks now.   I hold your favorite fluted
conch shell, smell its old salt-smell and listen to it speak of ocean absence.

The striated shell's inner surface spirals smooth, rose-pink as dawn glow.
It curves into dark emptiness, where I cannot see and do not want to go.

NURSING HOME BATH

I walk the wide hallway, pause
to peer through a narrow slant
of open door, marked "BATH."

The room, white on white: ceiling,
walls, floor, fixtures. Florescent
lights buzz down the surreal scene.

She sways, suspended in a lift,
as in a cage . . . naked, waiting
above the swirling water.

Short hair is feather-cut, skin
flaccid and bird-thin legs dangle.
Breasts hang pendulous as

deserted oriole nests in winter.
She shivers . . . her body-song,
a broken-wing requiem.

WILL DEATH BE THIS ?
A watercolor by Kate Hepburn
London, 2000

Blues, blues, in graduated hues, rise from the depths
of purple-blue ocean, across pale sand and upward
                                    to depths of blue-purple sky.

On the far right, two isosceles cypress trees wear dense
blue-green foliage, reach skyward in mature stature and
                                    stand as we, touching, waiting.

Will death be this . . . a simple easing from one world
to the next, a last wave of breath gliding like satin across
                                    endless sand to that other blue?

I move closer to the painting and discover a balustrade wall
blending color with blanched sand. Built long, strong and
                                    high, it separates ocean from sky.

THE NAMES QUILT

I watch you grow weak
as a stricken birch
leaning, black-
lesioned limbs
bare to break
fall to die
c a r v i n g
d o w n
e a r l y
snow
gro
un
d

legion is your name

unsleeping hands
can only stitch

eyes blur to salt

LAMENTATION

You cry a song of sorrow,
older than the blues;
I will bend to you, my love
and enter sorrow with you.

It consumes with smoldering fire
but I will soothe your coming pain
when lesions burn cinder-dark;
my touch is waiting, cool as rain.

It pierces with unending cold.
Death will come, we know not how
but I will lie beside you, warm you,
constant as our mutual vows.

It burdens with granite weight
pressing your lungs into death
but I will close your lightless eyes,
releasing you to new life's breath.

You cry a song of sorrow,
older than the blues;
I will bend to you, my love
and enter sorrow with you.

TO M., SUICIDE BY DROWNING

we do not hear
your dark
wound speak

your note
jagged pain
wed to sorrow

at the edge
water carves
a moon path

that breathes
silken white
and beckons

you shiver
on the cusp
balance lost

below, last
breath pushes
water sky

beyond time
a light path
shimmers

within time
your dark
wound speaks

BLUE EYES

At eighty one, Auntie Arlie holds a silver-
edged mirror in age-blotched hands.

She pulls wiry white hair straight back
and ponders how furrows have grown
to cheek canyons, how eye corners
pucker as though stitched, how flaccid
skin descends in folds on her neck.

Her identical twin died late last spring . . .
identical, but for the smoker's cough.

She aches for her sister's presence and
when storms of absence shatter, she finds
the morning mirror, looks into reflected
blue eyes and finds her other self.

TIME

Your face, fresh as a primrose blush,

is framed by thick auburn hair, and

your neck, supple as a willow branch

curves below denim sky; you

are spring, splashed sun-green.

Now, autumn light lingers your face

and like seasoned ash trees that know

the touch of time when branches

bare to bones, you are gold leaf

falling, to be intimate with earth.

MY FATHER'S WORDS

Redwing blackbirds
like onyx beads
set with crimson

wounds, are strung
along a telephone wire
like broken decades

of a rosary. Feathered
bodies listen, shudder
the dark message

my father speaks: *Come.*
Your mother's dying.

MY FATHER SPEAKS TO MY MOTHER
1981

You are dying and want to.

Fifty two years of marriage
come to this . . . our five sons and daughter
journey to your bed,
frame your white grave.

Depression years, five miscarriages,
hailed-out crops, good harvests
and work and work and work,
bonded us in daily vow and faith,
but . . . always a distance between us.

You soared the skies as artist,
as poet, while I am earthbound,
practical, a hybrid seed corn farmer.
Our roots, like fingers interlaced,
separate.

I tell the children,
your mother got
what she wanted

THROUGH DAUGHTER EYES

Window light weaves shadows
across her bed. Below the sheet, body
bones link like her pearl rosary.
Rib hands hold her.

She does not speak, each day
a kind of weaning.

Her bluish-hued fingers smooth a white cloud
of blanket brought from her bed at home. It
warms empty shoulders, is soft against cheek.
Her hand stills.

She raises her head slightly, looks beyond
the window, beyond green-willow light . . .

one last, torn piece of air.

MARVELOUS LIGHT

Life and death: they are one, at core entwined.
Rainer Maria Rilke

You bring me forth
from womb darkness
and I journey
into the light of birth.

The seasons of time revolve,
evolving our lives.
Evening comes and mourning;

I release you
from death darkness
and you journey
into the light of rebirth.

I SOUGHT MY FATHER'S ARMS

1945

In the farmhouse kitchen
just before supper.

I am thirteen, his only daughter
and he pushes my maturing body away.
I am lost . . .

for in younger years his arms drew me close;
callused hands stroked my dark, Dutch-bobbed hair;
his day's-end beard laughed and roughed my face.

1981

The farmhouse kitchen,
just before supper,
my mother dead that afternoon.

A hand-written love poem to my father is found
on my mother's nightstand. I read it aloud to him.
His grief releases in a sudden wrench of breath.

His arms bridge the years
and draw me close.

DIRECTIVES

When death closes,
wrap my shoulders
against the stone cold
with a warm woolen
shawl and leave his
given ring wedded to
my finger, diamond
lifeless in a locked box.

I will wait for his light
to open me, dazzling
down the silent dark.

FAINT GREEN FRAGRANCE

Tuesday, in their fifty-second
year of marriage, she died.

Wednesday, a gray cold
presses farmhouse windows,
creeps moldings, seeps
his arthritic bones.

Thursday, he studies
their garden. Tomato plants
tangle and wither, leaving
vines frost-shriveled.

Friday, after the funeral,
he limps to the garden, eases
down on his good knee and
pulls tomato stakes she set.

Saturday, he opens the closet
to find her garden work shirt.
Cradling it, he lies down
on her side of the bed . . .

faint, green-vine fragrance
living still.

EASTER SUNDAY MORNING

Dawn. I sit with the Easter lily
as with a friend. Five trumpets
flare and heavy fragrance wraps
the air around my face. I see
again the breath of incense, hear
the chanted *In Paradisum* at my
mother's funeral. White, linen
robe falls to the floor. I lie
in my room, as though a tomb,
light-filled.

IN REMEMBRANCE

1936

pain hushes the hospital room as shadow
shards slant across bleached sheets

a child's bed with high metal rails locks
me in a stark prison   Mama turns

to leave   *Stay with me, please stay*
I say and cling to her hand on the bed

she soothes my cheek,
smoothes the pillow and dipping a cloth

in cool water, places it on my fevered face
for a moment, pain escapes

1981

Mama is dead
and in my dream, we both know she is dead

light in her hospital room
wraps us in amber aura

her body begins to fade
stay with me, please stay, I say

her body forms again;   she whispers
I love you so . . . but I must . . .

flesh becomes transparent as air
thin white bones dissolve

YOUR PICTURE DATED, 1973

I touch your face under my magnifying
    glass and remember pale skin, translucent

as mother of pearl lifted to light. Still I feel
    the last brush of your cheek as we said

our goodbye that long, August afternoon.
    Bright color fades from your picture

as though scrimmed with a watercolor wash
    of aqua. Our farm kitchen shone

with aqua: wall oven, icebox, counter tops.
    Your dresses, aprons, coat and even

your bumbershoot flaunted its aqua flare.
    And now, your picture fades to this color.

Will you wear a gown of aqua iridescence
    when you come to me at death's first light?

GOING HOME

A Sunday in August. We gather to touch family.
My uncle embraces me. Leukemia pulses his veins
as chemo balds his head, bleaches his body
like a stripped, white oak.

I think of my father.   I saw him today . . . tied
to a wheelchair. Purple-blotched hands idle in his lap;
flakes of dry skin sifting from his face like light snow
through the north grove.

Since last year's family reunion, death has ravaged.
Two fathers severed from eleven children; grieving widows
embraced by storm and green-leaf memories.

This November night, my aunt's phone call.
I light a candle on our kitchen table, keep vigil for my uncle.

At 4:40 a.m. his life went dark.

VISITATION

I walk straight ahead, choose
not to see an old lady tied
to her wheelchair, crumpled
like empty clothes,
choose not to imagine pain
as an old man's arm flails
the table before him,
choose not to hear others mutter
suffering.

I go to my father's room,
past remnants of people scattered
like empty shells, leaning on crab-
footed canes, using start-and-stop
walkers. They slide snail feet,
inching wheelchair houses around
the square, to nowhere.

My father sits, twice tied
at shoulders and hips, staring
at a blank screen.
I wheel him to the dining room
where smoking is allowed.

After two cigarettes
and three thin cigars are smoked
without pause, he signs himself
absently, but perfectly,
from forehead to chest,
left shoulder to right.

TIMELY MISSION NURSING HOME
Buffalo Center, Iowa

A cloud-dappled morning in May
I drive to sit beside my father
and hold his thick farmer hands
folded in his lap, calluses peeled
away like layers of days.

This rain-drenched spring,
in the cemetery outside of town,
sleeping mounds are covered
over with white-blossom clover.

In the common room, my father lifts
his bowed head. Intense brown eyes
pierce mine in sudden clarity
and sighing he says, *I'm waiting*
for a bed to lie down in.

MY FATHER WAITS

December snow.

Unharvested corn fields
hunker down in bitter cold:
bleached, broken stalks,
rows of winter ravage.

March sun.

Sheathed ears rustle
their rough paper husks,
begin to hear south wind
whisper . . . *harvest nears*.

THE ICE STORM OF THE CENTURY

that November night kills
the ninety-year-old windmill.
Hired men said there was no sound.

In morning's ice-glazed light
the great windmill leans against
a small choke-cherry tree.

I see the empty sky twist open.
My father turns away,
no longer speaks.

On the day my father died
a new ice storm silenced
our world.

THE DAY MY FATHER DIED

A winter weary
hibiscus

Last week, one
pale green torch

plumped
like a cocoon

This morning
the corolla flares

orange-winged
butterfly

FROM MATER DOLOROSA CHURCH

my father's funeral procession moves west to Calvary Cemetery.
I walk to the mouth of the new grave.
Zero wind pries

my winter coat. I look deep into that final dark and remember
last June when he carried a bucket
of well water

for Mama's grave. He came to drench the geraniums he planted
on Memorial Day. I watched
as he knelt

on his good knee to mound dry loam around her wilted flowers.
He scooped water into the moat,
ladle by ladle.

Sorrow wrapped round our faces like summer's sultry breath.
His hand pulled hard against
her gravestone

as he rose, then bent to snap off old blossom spikes. Petals
clung, blood red. I winced
at the breaking.

EASTER ORATORIO

In our greening yard

April's first forsythia

bursts from slender

tombs . . . a fountain

cascading small,

four-petal blooms

of sun . . . spilled

hallelujah.

DIAMOND, OPAL, TURQUOISE, JADE

After her death, I write poems in my mother's
   orange velvet rocking chair where she wrote poems
      for years. Familiar arms holds me close.

On my fingers, four of her rings: an engagement
   diamond, accepted at age twenty-eight; a fire opal,
      Christmas gift from six children; a turquoise

oval set in silver, bought by my father on a trip
   to Arizona and a round, jade, made from a button
      given by her rock-hound, Colorado brother.

I touch these rings when beginning a poem and
   sense her presence in the marrow of these stones.

ON YOUR LOOM

my daughter
see the colors of a sunlit prism on your wall
enter its spectrum, find the path

where scarlet tulips lift their perfect goblet cups

where orange glory flowers blaze in dawn light

where yellow trumpet blooms amaze noon sun

where green orchid petals glide like satin clouds

where blue hydrangeas abide as close as family

where indigo wisteria offers wisps of fragrance

where violet hyacinths shiver above spring snow

where white lilies gift the air with silent alleluias

my daughter
weave words that shimmer a glissando
of color on your loom

IN MY MOTHER'S HOUSE

north of the farm
forty acres of *linum* flax bloom as pale blue sea
linen woven

in the buckwheat field
honeycomb hives buzz, rich with beeswax gold
candles molded

on County Road 134
an open pit yields crystalline, brown-sugar sand
china fired

in British Columbia
the Kimberley Mine offers veins of argentine ore
silverware formed

from Sonoma County
terraced vines cluster grapes, pressed to sweet juice
wine chilled

in a wildflower field
purple larkspur, yellow primrose and crimson clover
bouquet gathered

I hear you call, *Come,*
the table is set, the banquet prepared; we wait for you
I rise from dark

FULL MOON

His fingers touch my forehead creases
        hidden below white hair, follow cheek furrows
        forming parentheses around my mouth; thin
        wrinkles line upper lip and skin drapes, soft
        in neck pleats. I lean into his still strong hand
        remembering sun and green years . . . but now
        all eases downward, drawn toward waiting earth.

Yet . . . when a full moon opens the dark
        of our room, pouring thick cream light across
        the quilt made from variegated pieces of our life
        and when age-spotted hands see better than eyes,
        love comes young again, luminous as dawn.
        Our one breath rests on tender air and drifting
        into peace, sleep lasts long and deep.

THE THREAD STILL HOLDS

Before dying she spoke of her gift to me.
After her funeral, I return to the farm.

In an upstairs closet, her cedar chest
with one broken brass hinge, waits.

Next to the smooth, sanded bottom lay
my baby blanket, appliquéd and quilted

in a nine-square pattern of yellow calico
called, Sun Bonnet Sue. Some squares

were worn through, and the silky binding
frayed feather-thin from my fingers, yet

each patient, even stitch, set with white
cotton thread still counts ten to the inch.

About the Author

Born on a southern Minnesota farm, the only daughter in a family of five sons, she attended a one room schoolhouse for eight years, the local high school in Delavan and then earned a Bachelor of Arts degree in music at the College of St. Benedict. For the next twenty-six years, she was a full-time wife and mother, parenting seven children with her husband, Mark. She spent several years as a grade-school music teacher, overlapping with years as a guitarist and music minister at local parishes, plus eighteen years as an instructor for the Diocesan Family Life Bureau. The poetry muse whispered to her in 1989 while attending a course in bibliotherapy. Currently she works in the St. Cloud Hospital's "Recovery Plus" Program as a facilitator of poetry therapy. Each poem in *Quilt Pieces* connects intimate details of three generations of family life . . . joining the fragments to form the whole.